The Elder Scrolls V

SKYRIM

TAROT DECK
GUIDEBOOK

WRITTEN BY
Tori Schafer

ILLUSTRATED BY
Erika Hollice

TITAN
BOOKS
LONDON

CONTENTS

INTRODUCTION

Every Dragonborn begins their adventure as a prisoner. From riding in rickety wagons to escaping fire-breathing Dragons, the Dragonborn is thrust into the world of Skyrim, where a thousand paths lie ahead. But that beginning resonates with every player. After all, do we not often feel trapped by something in our lives, awaiting the fortuitous moment of our escape so that our adventure may begin?

The *Skyrim Tarot Deck and Guidebook* is here to guide you through whatever journey you may be on. Whether you face a horde of Dragons or the first day of a new job, it never hurts to reflect on what was, what is, and what will be. The cards in this deck will help you do just that. Use them to seek answers within the past, present, or future.

You may approach tarot cards for different reasons. Perhaps you wish to reflect on a difficult situation. Perhaps it's a fun pastime you share with friends and family. Or perhaps you believe that the deck can peer into the future and warn you of what is to come. Whatever the reason, remember that no future is set in stone. Your deck is merely there to warn you of possible hardships or help you realize possible opportunities within your journey. It lies within you to decide how best to meet that fate.

The *Skyrim Tarot Deck and Guidebook* is filled with iconic characters, places, and themes carefully selected to convey archetypal meanings within the original tarot deck. This guidebook provides explanations for both the upright and reversed aspects of all cards. The final chapter includes sample spreads for future readings.

Now, let us journey forth into the heart of Skyrim.

UNDERSTANDING YOUR TAROT DECK

If you're new to tarot cards, your deck may seem intimidating at first. Seventy-eight cards, each with a special meaning? Not to mention that meaning may change depending on whether the card is upright or reversed! Have no fear, brave adventurer. This guide comes with a tutorial level.

The first twenty-two cards in a deck are called the Major Arcana. They represent significant events in your life with a lasting impact. These cards also speak of a journey of sorts as you read them in order. The cards are numbered zero to XXI, starting with The Fool, who is filled with limitless possibilities. Their journey will see them gather Strength and Fortune, face Justice, and overcome Death. And after many hardships and enriching experiences, they shall be granted the enlightenment of The World. Not too unlike the Dragonborn, wouldn't you say?

The remaining fifty-six cards make up the Minor Arcana, which describe everyday situations and people in your life. The cards are divided into four suits: Spells, Lockpicks, Arms, Voice. (The tarot-initiated may know them as the traditional Wands, Coins, Swords, and Cups. This deck takes those ideas and adds a Skyrim-flavored twist.) The Minor Arcana cards are numbered 1 through 10, with four additional court cards in each suit that represent a Page, a Knight, a Queen, and a King.

VII

The Chariot

King of Voice

King of Spells

Page of Lockpicks

Queen of Arms

Knight of Voice

The Suit of Spells represents adventure, creativity, and inspiration. The members of its court, represented by the Mages Guild, are courageous and passionate. It corresponds with the element fire.

The Suit of Lockpicks represents finance, earthly materials, and laborious pursuits. The members of its court, represented by the Thieves Guild, are hardworking and reliable. It corresponds with the element earth.

The Suit of Arms represents conflict, power, and judgment. The members of its court, represented by the Companions, are powerful and keen. It corresponds with the element wind.

The Suit of Voice represents emotions, relationships, and imagination. The members of its court, represented in our deck by the Greybeards, are creative and harmonious. It corresponds with the element water.

Before we continue, a note on the gender expression within tarot readings. Many cards are represented by the women and men of Skyrim, but these cards are not limited to the gender binary. You may find that the Queen of Arms reminds you of your father, or the Emperor is reminiscent of a nonbinary friend. Although the card descriptions are traditionally masculine or feminine, they can be interpreted freely across many different gender expressions. The cards are here to fit your personal journey, whatever that may be.

MAJOR ARCANA

THE FOOL

The Fool represents the beginning of a journey and the desire to accomplish a great goal. Like the Fool, Cicero journeys to Skyrim in order to find the last Dark Brotherhood sanctuary. His goal is to find a Listener who can speak with the Night Mother and carry out her murderous desires. You may be starting a similar journey in your life, though perhaps with fewer assassinations involved.

UPRIGHT

Though Cicero's beliefs may be dark in nature, they carry him forward without hesitation. So, too, must you begin your journey. Allow your belief in your goal to guide you into the unknown. The goal that lies ahead will be well worth the effort.

REVERSED

Though Cicero journeys to Skyrim to protect the Night Mother, his foolishness and rash decisions lead to the Dark Brotherhood turning against him. Do not follow in his footsteps. Make sure to carefully plan the journey that lies ahead. As they say, only a fool rushes in.

THE MAGICIAN

Farengar Secret-Fire is the court wizard to Jarl Balgruuf and master of many magical arts. He has gained control over the arcane and is able to take that knowledge and manifest it into spells and enchanted items. For those looking to master their own arts, you would do well to follow his good example.

UPRIGHT

You have demonstrated the will, mastery, and control to learn a new art or talent. Whether you wish to understand fiery spells or begin a new hobby, learn from Farengar's dedication to his craft. To gain a new skill, you must have the will to keep at it.

REVERSED

Not everyone has Farengar's single-minded dedication. You may find yourself faltering in your study of a new skill. Remember to take a breath, consider your options, and perhaps go and fight some bandits. The enchanting table will still be waiting when you wish to return.

THE HIGH PRIESTESS

The High Priestess is the link between the seen and unseen, desire and manifestation, spiritual and physical. Saint Alessia, liberator of mankind and founder of the Eight Divines, embodies these principles like no other in Tamriel lore. From her teachings, we can learn to bridge the gap between what we wish and what we make reality.

UPRIGHT

You have gained Alessia's blessings and made your will into reality. Though you may not topple regimes and establish empires, your desires will surely be made manifest. Through this revelation, you have gained a better understanding of yourself and your journey.

REVERSED

Alessia's path was not an easy one, and neither is yours. You may find yourself hesitating, unsure of what you want. Perhaps you lack the power to make your desires into reality. Take some time to reflect on what may be holding you back from your ambitions.

THE EMPRESS

The Empress rules over her domain with a nurturing heart, allowing her kingdoms and people to prosper. Elisif the Fair exemplifies this quality in her governance of Solitude following her late husband's death. She wishes for her city and people to flourish under her rule and has taken power in order to make this so. And so, too, can you.

UPRIGHT

Jarl Elisif works endlessly in order for Solitude to thrive, and it seems you have taken inspiration from her hard work. Your dedication shall lead to prosperous ends, whether it be in your career, creative endeavors, or household. Look forward to the sweet fruits of your labor.

REVERSED

It is not always easy being empress—or jarl, for that matter. Elisif must concede much of her power to the Empire. Although she wishes for prosperity, she is insecure in her ability to maintain it. Are there aspects of your life where that you feel insecure? What can you do to make them flourish once more?

THE EMPEROR

The Emperor is the ultimate authority over his dominion. High King Torygg once ruled over Skyrim, working tirelessly to ensure its safety. But many questioned his loyalty to his homeland. Did he work with the Empire to guarantee peace, or was he too frightened of war?

UPRIGHT

Even after his death, many Nords considered Torygg a wise and just leader. Follow his example as you take your own position of leadership. Be just in your decisions and firm in your conviction. The strength of your authority comes from the strength of your resolve.

REVERSED

Many question Torygg's loyalty to Skyrim, believing him to be a puppet of the Empire. You may have experienced a similar loss of control over some aspect of your life. Evaluate where you feel powerless and what circumstances led you there. Can you rise up against such challenges, or will you fall to a mightier power as Torygg did? It is up to you to decide.

THE HIEROPHANT

The Hierophant conforms to society and upholds tradition, whether that be cultural practices, religion, or written law. These ideals are upheld by Julianos, one of the Divines, in the land of Tamriel. He is a god of literature, law, history, and contradiction. Will you follow his ways? Or will you strike out on a path all your own?

UPRIGHT

Julianos is pleased by your adherence to tradition. Convention and societal norms have a strong hold over your life. Reflect on how these traditions impact your journey and how they may aid or hinder you. Are you guided by convention, or forced to heed it?

REVERSED

Though Julianos is the god of many things, his rule over contradiction stands out most. Do you find yourself breaking away from tradition in some way? Know that you, too, are a child of Julianos. Hold tight to your convictions. We are not all destined to walk the path society has laid before us.

THE LOVERS

The Lovers represent harmony between opposing factors, such as the inner and outer aspects of life. The Battle-Born and Gray-Mane families maintain a bitter rivalry, one family supporting the Empire and the other supporting the Stormcloak Rebellion. But the love between Jon and Olfina signifies that even such opposition can be overcome.

UPRIGHT

Jon and Olfina desire each other despite their family's rivalry. They have overcome their different viewpoints and found love. You may be tempted by something as well, whether it be a person or desire itself. A choice lies before you. Can you achieve balance?

REVERSED

Do not allow temptation to get the better of you. Take the time to stabilize your emotions and think carefully on your choices. Jon and Olfina must keep their love a secret from their families, lest they be torn apart. Learn from their careful actions and do not rush ahead. After all, love can often be blind.

THE CHARIOT

The Chariot moves forever toward its goal, often without heed of how far the destination is. Arvak, the undead mount found within the Soul Cairn, endlessly runs toward an unknown destination. Not even death can stop his journey. Can you take the reins?

UPRIGHT

Arvak is a tireless mount, able to be endlessly summoned as the need arises. So, too, are your continual efforts toward whatever goal is set before you. Keep up your steady pace, for your destination lies ahead, not behind. With time, you will surely reach your goal.

REVERSED

Sometimes the path ahead truly is as endless as it seems. Arvak runs tirelessly in death without a clear direction or stopping point. Is your path the right one? Are you on the right track to meet your goals? Take the time to consider what lies ahead and how best to tackle it. Sometimes you lose sight of the destination on such a long journey.

STRENGTH

Strength allows us to overcome all obstacles, to rise above any challenge and tackle it head-on. It was by this strength that Ulfric Stormcloak overcame the Empire and saved Skyrim from foreign rule. Have you the will to follow his example, or will you abuse such power?

UPRIGHT

Rebelling against the Empire was no easy feat, given the might of its armies and vast resources. But Ulfric found the strength to overcome these obstacles, gathering his people and leading them to victory. You, too, have it within you to find the strength to overcome your current challenges and prevail.

REVERSED

Sometimes our strength leads to destructive ends. To many, Ulfric's quest for power did not always seem fair or just. Do not allow your own power to become abusive and tyrannical. Know that strength will lead to destruction, have you not the understanding to use it justly.

THE HERMIT

The Hermit gains wisdom through reflection and isolation, and there is no greater example of this ideal than the Dragon Paarthurnax. Perched atop the Throat of the World, he worked to guide the Greybeards' monastic order and teach the Way of the Voice. Heed his wisdom, for in it may lie the answers you seek in your own quest.

UPRIGHT

Paarthurnax guides the Dragonborn on their journey to master their power and defeat Alduin. So, too, must you listen to the wisdom of those more experienced than yourself. Their advice will guide you toward greater enlightenment.

REVERSED

What a different road the Dragonborn would have followed had they refused the wisdom of Paarthurnax and rejected their destiny. You may find your current responsibilities overwhelming and refuse to heed the advice of others. Do not give in to such temptations. There is wisdom to be gained, if only you will listen.

THE WHEEL
OF FORTUNE

The Wheel of Fortune tells us that sometimes our fates are out of our hands. Olava the Feeble knows this better than most, for though she can see the future, she has not the means to change it. Will she bring you good tidings, adventurer? Or does misfortune loom ahead?

UPRIGHT

Just as Olava spoke to the Dragonborn of awaiting treasure, so, too, does good fortune await you. Look forward to an unexpected stroke of good luck or success in a current endeavor. But remember, good luck is only as helpful as you are prepared for it to be.

REVERSED

Olava has seen misfortune in your future, but that does not mean you cannot endure. You may fail an enterprise or suffer a setback. Do not allow this to dishearten you. Just as the Dragonborn overcomes many obstacles over the course of their adventure, so can you.

JUSTICE

Justice is the card of equality, fair rule, and balance. Talos, the hero turned emperor turned god, embodies these ideals. It was through his rule that Tamriel was united under one empire, and through his godhood that mankind knew governance. Is justice on your side today?

UPRIGHT

Talos has decreed that justice shall be done. You will find the injustices against you righted or shall earn your just reward for services rendered. Remember that in all things, balance is required. Might must be tempered with kindness, the body supplemented with the mind.

REVERSED

Talos does not favor you this day. You will be met with injustice or unfairness. But do not lose faith, for you shall prevail. Use mercy and understanding when judging others, and avoid severity. Godhood is not obtained through bitterness, but rather through the power to rise above.

THE HANGED MAN

Between decision and indecision, the Hanged Man is held. He has been suspended by inner conflict, or perhaps a mere twist of fate. Esbern exemplifies this dilemma through his duties as a member of the Blades. His once-proud order is broken, but he still has duties to fulfill. He simply awaits the right time. And sometimes, so must you.

UPRIGHT

There is a matter in which you feel at a crossroads, unable to turn back yet unable to move forward. Take this time to reflect on what lies ahead and what you might lose, just as Esbern awaited the Dragonborn's return. This time of respite will give you greater insight into your current situation.

REVERSED

You fight against the need for respite, even though your path forward is blocked. Do not allow your arrogance to lead to wasted efforts. Esbern waited until the return of the Dragonborn to continue his duties as a member of the Blades. A similar moment shall arrive to open your path, but that time is not quite yet.

DEATH

Sithis is known throughout Tamriel to embody death. Neither Divine nor Daedra, good nor bad. He is simply the void from which all things came and to which all things will return. Do not fear his presence, for it is only through death that we may be reborn.

UPRIGHT

You have accepted the teachings of Sithis and readied yourself for a transformation, perhaps spiritual or material. There will be great destruction followed by great renewal. Be open to new ideas and new opportunities, for through them you will better yourself.

REVERSED

You have rejected the wisdom of Sithis, and thus your journey stagnates. Perhaps you fear such change, for what is more frightening than the unknown? Look inward and seek the truth. Do you wish to remain unchanging? Or do you seek the renewal that Sithis offers?

TEMPERANCE

Temperance is not merely about the balance between material and spiritual, but also about the ability to adapt in order to maintain that balance. Sotha Sil has taken this creed to a godly level, adapting himself through both magical and technological means. Can you find balance in your own journey?

UPRIGHT

When Sotha Sil achieved godhood, he chose to master both technological wonders and magical feats. You have learned from his wisdom and shall find balance within your life as well, whether it be material and spiritual, career and home, or spells and swordsmanship.

REVERSED

Balance is not so easily achieved. Near the end of his life, Sotha Sil began to crave perfection, locking himself away and modifying his body to gross extents. Do not allow yourself to become similarly obsessed with but one aspect of your life. Imbalance will lead to naught but disaster.

THE DEVIL

The Devil is the great tempter in many stories, and there is no greater temptress in Tamriel than Mephala. She is known to seduce mortals to destructive ends and holds dominion over lies, secrets, sex, and murder. Will you allow yourself to fall to her whispered temptations?

UPRIGHT

You have fallen into Mephala's webs of lies and deceit, allowing material pleasures to surpass the need for spiritual ones. Take heed of your vices and acknowledge their destructive potential. It is not too late to overcome the Webspinner's whispers.

REVERSED

You have overcome temptation and are on the path to recovery. Spiritual understanding has begun to awaken within you, though it may yet be weak. Know that all bonds can be broken, even the sticky webs of Mephala. Hold strong and continue your path to enlightenment.

THE TOWER

The Tower represents chaos and conflict, and there's no greater lover of such insanity than the Daedric Prince Sheogorath. Master of mania and dementia, his realm embodies hardships that can fell even the mightiest. Will you be among the fallen?

UPRIGHT

Sheogorath has chosen you, and that is never a good thing. There is great chaos in your life, leading to conflict and strife. You find your plans disrupted by either an outside force or your own inability. Take heed of Sheogorath's influence and reflect. How can you escape his mad realm?

REVERSED

You have freed yourself from Sheogorath's madness, but at great cost. You may find yourself exhausted by such an ordeal and unable to return to normalcy just yet. Allow yourself time to heal before beginning your journey anew. You have earned a respite.

THE STAR

The Star is a symbol of hope even in the darkest of nights. And what better deity to herald that hope than the Lady of Dusk and Dawn? Through Azura's will, heroes are guided and races are born. Will you follow her light through the darkness?

UPRIGHT

Azura has brought hope and inspiration in your darkest hour. Look forward to great love and aid after a long night. But know that Azura can only guide you through the dusk. It must be within your strength to follow her into a hopeful dawn.

REVERSED

Doubt and pessimism have blinded you to Azura's blessing. You cannot see the stars beyond the dark night. Take heed of this, and reflect on what is. Are your troubles truly endless, with no hope in sight? Every dusk eventually breaks into dawn. Do not lose hope.

THE MOON

The Moon hangs bright in the dark sky, offering both intuition and illusions. Nocturnal, prince of night, darkness, and luck, is much like that mysterious Moon, for her favors come with a price. Will you gain the blessing of the Night Mistress, or is the light of the Moon merely peril in disguise?

UPRIGHT

Nocturnal proves to be a tricky mistress. Your intuition and imagination lead you forward, but be wary of their deceiving light. Hidden perils and unknown foes lurk before you. Can you outsmart them before they outsmart you?

REVERSED

Nocturnal offers her mastery over luck and darkness. Your intuition will lead you down the right path, and all suffering shall be weathered. You must be prepared to render payment, however. No prince's blessing comes without a price.

THE SUN

The Sun is filled with life and energy, the purview of the Daedric Prince Meridia. Through her guidance is happiness obtained, as she takes great joy in rewarding mortals who protect the realm of man. Perhaps she will wish to reward your efforts as well.

UPRIGHT

Meridia smiles on you this day and has given you great blessings of joy. Expect well-earned victories and honored achievements in your future. Still, do not think such gifts are given lightly. It is only by your dedication that Meridia's favor is granted.

REVERSED

Meridia has not blessed your future. Be wary of troubles, losses, and broken promises. But do not lose hope, for there is not just one adventure in this life. Your next quest will surely see a brighter sun.

JUDGMENT

Judgment is a card given only to those who deserve it, whether for good or ill. In that same vein, Mjoll the Lioness passes judgment over what she believes is wrong and right. She wishes to aid the righteous and condemn the wicked. Which are you?

UPRIGHT

Just as Mjoll wishes the world to be just, so is your future. Your labor has borne fruit, and your rewards are plentiful and freely attained. This great bounty comes with a greater understanding of yourself and your place in the world.

REVERSED

An unfavorable judgment lies before you. Your missteps have led to failure, and you now risk losing something precious. Look at what you have reaped and ask what you have sown. Have you truly been the hero Mjoll would wish to aid?

THE WORLD

The World represents all that is and all that will be, a connection and deeper understanding of the universe and your place within it. Such is the knowledge of Akatosh, Dragon god of time. Just as he encompasses endurance, invincibility, and everlasting legitimacy, so, too, can you.

UPRIGHT

The World has been found within you, and Akatosh has granted his blessing. Your journey is now complete, and you have been rewarded not only with triumph but also with a deeper connection to both the spiritual and material.

REVERSED

Perhaps you fear your journey's end, or perhaps you lack the conviction to see it through. Whatever the case, Akatosh cannot yet share his wisdom with you. Reflect on where your journey has taken you. Why are you hesitant for it to end?

MINOR ARCANA

SUIT OF SPELLS

King of Spells

KING OF SPELLS (SAVOS AREN)

Upright: The King of Spells is an experienced mage and capable of powerful magic. He honors those who show great promise and will aid your journey in discovering or mastering a skill. Look toward his work as a shining example.

Reversed: The King has become a mage too self-obsessed with magic to see the worth of any other discipline. He will ruthlessly try to force your interests to match his own and sees no values in skills he does not already possess.

Queen of Spells

QUEEN OF SPELLS (MIRABELLE ERVINE)

Upright: The Queen of Spells nurtures and empowers her domain, whether that be the Mages Guild or your workplace. She will guide you to greater power, though she may seek your aid in return. Help her homestead flourish, and you will find her to be a faithful companion.
Reversed: The domineering Queen cares little for those around her. In pursuit of her own power, she will not hesitate to abuse those she commands. Be careful of her callousness.

Knight of Spells

KNIGHT OF SPELLS
(WUUNFERTH THE UNLIVING)

Upright: The Knight of Spells is passionate about the magic he possesses, though that passion can lead to arrogance. He may be quick to dismiss those who are not so magically (or perhaps artistically) inclined. Still, his wisdom and aid should not be rebuked.

Reversed: The Knight's arrogance has become his undoing, leading to discord and frustrations in your life. Beware his interference with your own work and passions.

Page of Spells

PAGE OF SPELLS (TOLFDIR)

Upright: The Page of Spells is passionate in what he does, though he does not require praise or power in order to pursue that passion. He will be your steadfast peer as you learn your spells and will give honest advice on how you can increase your skills.

Reversed: The Page has become domineering and unstable. He will hinder your passions and may even lead you to hate what you once loved. Beware his cruel influence.

Ace of Spells

ACE OF SPELLS

Upright: Your adventure begins! Prepare for a new journey, whether that be a creative endeavor, a career choice, or simply a new chapter of your life.
Reversed: Your adventure has been delayed, forcing you to cancel plans or defer your journey. Take this time to reflect on the setback and how you can overcome it.

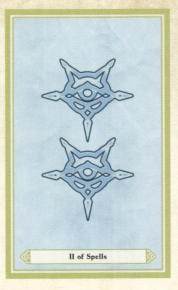

II of Spells

II OF SPELLS

Upright: You have been emboldened to set out on a new enterprise. Do not allow this opportunity to pass you by! Every journey starts with that first quest.

Reversed: You fear an upcoming change in your life and are too timid to take the first step. Check your stats to determine what you may be lacking for the quest ahead.

III of Spells

III OF SPELLS

Upright: You have established your power and found companions to fight by your side. Do not allow this strength to become arrogance. The next dungeon may be more difficult than you think!

Reversed: Beware of treachery among those you consider friends. Their help may lead to hardship, whether that be a loss of power or material goods. Keep a close eye on your inventory!

IV of Spells

IV OF SPELLS

Upright: You have completed a difficult quest and will be rewarded. Take this time to rest and recover. This peace and good fortune have been justly earned.

Reversed: A rarity among your deck, the reversed position of this card holds the same meaning as its upright variant. Though your rewards may not attain such high tiers, they shall be rewards nonetheless.

V OF SPELLS

Upright: An enemy approaches! Prepare for combat and conflict, for an obstacle has blocked your path. Remember that fortune favors the bold.

Reversed: An opportunity appears before you, whether it be a new friendship, career path, or character class. Your victory is assured.

VI of Spells

VI OF SPELLS

Upright: Victory is close at hand, despite the hardships you have endured. Expect good news and decisive successes. Your companions may help in this victory.

Reversed: Your rewards will be delayed, and victory may go to your enemy. Do not allow their good fortune to hinder yours. Take the time to drink a potion of healing and live to fight another day.

VII of Spells

VII OF SPELLS

Upright: A competition lies before you, and only through courage do you dare hope to succeed. Keep your sword and spells at the ready, and victory is assured.

Reversed: Your indecisiveness will get the better of you. Do not hesitate in the face of danger, lest you end up a Frostbite Spider's dinner.

VIII of Spells

VIII OF SPELLS

Upright: You are approaching the end of a long quest line, and your reward lies just ahead. Do not be hasty! The end boss still awaits, and you must be prepared to defeat it.

Reversed: Your journey has been delayed. Beware of stagnation during your quest, whether it be in business or relationships.

IX of Spells

IX OF SPELLS

Upright: The time has come for a moment's rest during a great struggle. Take the opportunity to learn a few spells or buy better armor before heading back into the dungeon.

Reversed: You have overtaxed yourself and grown weak. You are underleveled for your current struggle, and the obstacles ahead may be too great to overcome.

X of Spells

X OF SPELLS

Upright: Your power has been used unwisely, and the burden you carry is great. Still, your journey shall soon come to an end. Be prepared for a final trial before your quest line is finished.

Reversed: Though your battle may be hard-fought, you are on the path toward defeat. Prepare to suffer a great loss or setback. Take time to reflect how best to tackle your next quest.

SUIT OF LOCKPICKS

King of Lockpicks

KING OF LOCKPICKS
(MERCER FREY)

Upright: Master among thieves, leader of guilds, the King of Lockpicks is at the top of his industry. His work ethic is sound, his skills reliable, and he is always savvy in his finances.

Reversed: A King filled with vice and immoral cunning is liable to cheat and scheme at every opportunity. He will stop at nothing to gain his power, including stabbing you in the back.

Queen of Lockpicks

QUEEN OF LOCKPICKS (VEX)

Upright: The Queen of Lockpicks is a talented individual who watches over her domain. She will use her keen skills to aid those she deems worthy of her protection.

Reversed: The Queen has become paranoid of those she once trusted, and her suspicions have left her duties neglected. Beware her dependence on others, especially yourself, as she may push her duties onto you.

Knight of Lockpicks

KNIGHT OF LOCKPICKS (BRYNJOLF)

Upright: The Knight of Lockpicks is a guild man through and through. He is upright in his duties, and his aid is reliable. Know that you can trust him with any matter, though he may never rise to power.

Reversed: The Knight has stagnated, refusing to progress or grow as an individual. Do not allow his carelessness to hinder your own progress. Though you may share his duties, that's no reason to share his poor work ethic.

Page of Lockpicks

PAGE OF LOCKPICKS (SAPPHIRE)

Upright: The Page of Lockpicks is ready to learn new ideas at every turn, honing her skills and mastering many arts. She is careful about her affairs and may be hard to grow close to.

Reversed: The Page has become too obsessed with worldly goods, leading to excess and wastefulness. Do not allow her self-indulgent ways to hinder your own financial interests.

Ace of Lockpicks

ACE OF LOCKPICKS

Upright: The time has come for a new great heist. This marks the beginning of wealth and material rewards, combined with prosperity and great contentment.

Reversed: Your heist was a bust, and your material rewards have been delayed. This may be due to miserliness or greed, either in yourself or another.

II of Lockpicks

II OF LOCKPICKS

Upright: You have the ability to balance two aspects of your life, such as work and home. This has led to happiness and harmony, though new projects may be difficult to begin at this time.

Reversed: Your life is imbalanced, and you have a hard time juggling different projects. It may be time to clear out your journal and abandon a few quests to focus on what truly matters.

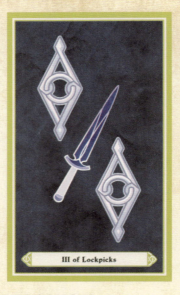

III of Lockpicks

III OF LOCKPICKS

Upright: You have gained greater understanding of your craft, whether it be lockpicking, finances, or some related skill. Your hard work has led to increased rewards.

Reversed: Your lack of skills and ignorance of your craft have led to frustrations and failed starts. Know that proficiency comes with time and experience, not mere desire.

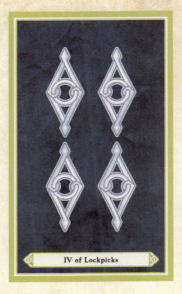

IV of Lockpicks

IV OF LOCKPICKS

Upright: Your latest heists have increased your wealth, though there is little to be found beyond these material rewards. This fortune may ultimately lead to greed and miserliness.

Reversed: An unexpected loss in fortune has dealt you a series of setbacks. Beware impulsive purchases and a loss of ambition. Do you really need that new set of armor?

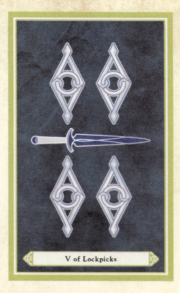

V of Lockpicks

V OF LOCKPICKS

Upright: Watch out for the loss of material comforts, perhaps through unemployment or unexpected debts. Keep an eye out for conflict within your guild (or workplace). Trouble may be brewing.

Reversed: New employment or fortune is gained after renewed toil. You shall recover from a great loss, whether that be an empty vault or a demotion at work. Be thankful for the charity of others.

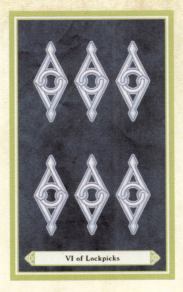

VI of Lockpicks

VI OF LOCKPICKS

Upright: Your hard work shall be justly rewarded, as will the hard work of your allies. Look forward to sharing in great fortune with your companions.

Reversed: Beware your debts to others and a lack of charity from those who may owe you in turn. Others may be jealous of your fortune and seek to steal it away.

VII of Lockpicks

VII OF LOCKPICKS

Upright: Your trusty lockpicks have failed during the most critical heist. Your latest enterprise will come to a halt. Expect a loss in fortune and disappointment in a current endeavor.

Reversed: Every vault you pick open has little to offer. Despite your best efforts, only a small reward will be gained after your hard work. This may lead to frustration over your current endeavors.

VIII of Lockpicks

VIII OF LOCKPICKS

Upright: You will begin a new trade or profession, or perhaps find new employment in your current field. The apprentice thief is on their way to becoming master of the guild.

Reversed: Your ambitions are in danger of failure. Setbacks have led to frustration, which has hindered development in a field or skill. Take a breath. Picking certain locks requires time.

IX of Lockpicks

IX OF LOCKPICKS

Upright: Enjoy comfort in the home you have created. You have attained wisdom in your crafts and the capacity for great love of your surroundings. Truly a stockpile to covet.

Reversed: You face a possible loss of comfort and possessions. Be wary of thieves and unexpected failure. Now is the time to move with caution, for stealth shall always be your ally.

X of Lockpicks

X OF LOCKPICKS

Upright: Great riches and inheritance shall be yours to claim. Your house or business will prosper after much hard work. A trove to make the Thieves Guild proud.

Reversed: Your guild will suffer a great loss, whether due to burdensome coworkers or unexpected misfortune. Be cautious of projects with high risk.

SUIT OF ARMS

King of Arms

KING OF ARMS
(KODLAK WHITEMANE)

Upright: The King of Arms is a wise leader who ends disputes and builds companionship. He seeks to hone your potential and will give sage advice in any conflict you may be a part of. Look toward him in times of discord.

Reversed: The King has grown harsh and malicious. He will start endless disputes with all who dare oppose him and will drag you into conflict as well. Beware his barbarity.

Queen of Arms

QUEEN OF ARMS
(AELA THE HUNTRESS)

Upright: The Queen of Arms is a keen and intelligent woman who knows when to be kind and when to be firm. She will give you strength in times of distress, guiding you through crushing losses and bitter sorrows.

Reversed: The Queen has become pernicious and unreliable. She is given to jealousy and gossip and will deceive you for her own benefit. Beware her venomous promises.

Knight of Arms

KNIGHT OF ARMS (SKJOR)

Upright: The Knight of Arms is a dashing warrior, though he may come across as arrogant at times. He's quick to jump headfirst into conflict when he feels he must.

Reversed: The Knight has grown domineering, lording himself over those he deems weaker. He is quick to instigate conflict and will try to taunt you into meaningless fights. Do not let him.

Page of Arms

PAGE OF ARMS (FARKAS))

Upright: Loyal to a fault, the Page of Arms is an upright young warrior who knows the limits of his own strength. He will try to end conflicts whenever possible, though his attempts may seem clumsy.

Reversed: The Page has turned out to be cunning and frivolous and is possibly faking his goodwill toward you. Be prepared for his betrayal and the conflict that ensues because of it.

Ace of Arms

ACE OF ARMS

Upright: Your conquest begins as you set forth to triumph over a great evil, whether that be deadly Dragons or an unfair manager. Know that you will overcome that which seeks to hinder you.

Reversed: You have begun a conquest to disastrous results. Your obstacles have escalated, and you may have suffered a great loss. Take the time to gain a few levels before continuing your fight.

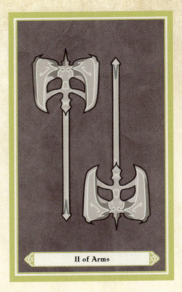

II of Arms

II OF ARMS

Upright: A current conflict has come to a stalemate, with neither side a clear winner. This may lead to tensions in your relationships with others. A direction must be chosen.

Reversed: A stalemate has come to an end, though the outcome may not be favorable. Watch carefully for those who may betray your trust.

III of Arms

III OF ARMS

Upright: Troubled times lie ahead for you. You may encounter rocky relationships, quarreling, or a negative change in your life. Be prepared to face these battles with your sword drawn.

Reversed: This card is rare in that the reversed position still foretells upheaval and conflict, though to a lesser degree than the upright variant.

IV of Arms

IV OF ARMS

Upright: Your battle has come to an end, and now is the time for rest. Your luck will soon change for the better, and you will be released from your present anxieties.

Reversed: The time has come to take up arms, for a great challenge awaits you. Prepare for this new quest with renewed caution. Rushing in will only lead to undue strife.

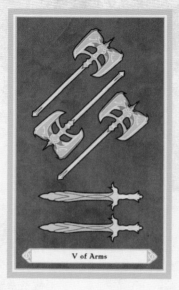

V of Arms

V OF ARMS

Upright: You have been unsuccessful in an endeavor and now face defeat. Prepare to meet unfairness, cruelty, and slander. This enemy has proved too great to slay.

Reversed: Your hubris may lead to defeat, or perhaps an empty victory. This battle will leave you feeling hollow and at a loss. No rewards will be granted for this quest.

VI of Arms

VI OF ARMS

Upright: Your battle will bring you new success and new journeys. Look toward the future for better opportunities. Anxieties will turn to peace, and new understanding will be found.

Reversed: Your current battle has you locked into place, unable to move forward in your quest. It may be prudent to seek other opportunities and build your strength before continuing this fight.

VII of Arms

VII OF ARMS

Upright: Your current strategy will fail you. Your unstable efforts will lead to defeat or perhaps a partial success. Alliances you once relied on may now fracture.
Reversed: You will receive sound advice that may lead to unexpected good, should you be wise enough to follow it. Your quest will be finished, though perhaps not in the way you expect.

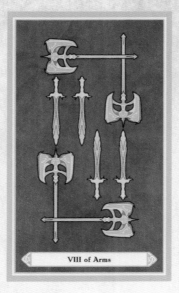

VIII of Arms

VIII OF ARMS

Upright: You feel imprisoned in your current situation and unable to escape. This may be due to fate or your own hesitation. Do you fear freedom?

Reversed: Chains that once held you are now broken. You are free to start your journey, whatever it may be. You have overcome your fears, even when faced with great Dragons.

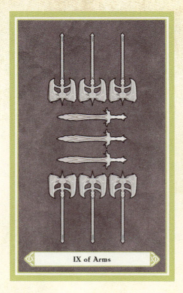

IX of Arms

IX OF ARMS

Upright: Beware a great setback in your future, leading to doubt and isolation. You may be given a heavy burden or exploited by those who hold power over you.

Reversed: Be patient, for your wounds are many. The time has come to drink a potion or see a healer before heading to your next quest. Your adventure can wait.

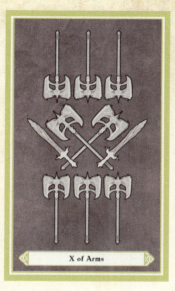

X of Arms

X OF ARMS

Upright: Your projects and plans are in danger of falling into ruin. Trouble will come to you despite careful planning and accumulated power. The unexpected shall be your downfall.

Reversed: You shall overcome a great evil and find victory after a long battle. But to do so, you must find the courage to stand and fight.

SUIT OF VOICE

King of Voice

KING OF VOICE (JURGEN WIND-CALLER)

Upright: The King of Voice seeks peace above all else, mastering his emotions and leading others with benevolence and kindness. He will always take full responsibility for his duties, even when the burden is great.

Reversed: Though the King may appear calm, under this facade lies a cruel and crafty nature. He will attempt to deceive you for his own ends. Do not let him.

Queen of Voice

QUEEN OF VOICE (KYNE)

Upright: The Queen of Voice always seeks to protect those who need her aid. She is a devoted woman who will lead you to success with loyalty and kindness.

Reversed: Though this Queen may seem intelligent, she has no kindness in her heart. Do not rely on her, for her dishonesty will hinder your successes.

Knight of Voice

KNIGHT OF VOICE (ARNGEIR)

Upright: The Knight of Voice is filled with hope and wishes for harmony above all. He may invite you to a new endeavor, whether that be a career path, hobby, or relationship.

Reversed: The Knight has become too focused on himself to aid others and may seek to trick you. Look closely at his invitations, for they hold naught but deceit.

Page of Voice

PAGE OF VOICE (EINARTH)

Upright: The Page of Voice will aid the next step of your journey, not as a leader but as a peer. He will encourage you to reflect on your adventure and seek new opportunities.

Reversed: The Page has little desire to take his own journey, much less encourage anyone else. He may become an obstacle, enticing you to join him in his slothful ways.

Ace of Voice

ACE OF VOICE

Upright: This marks the beginning of a great emotional awakening, either with others or within yourself. Divine power will fill your voice, and from that, your life will brim with joy, contentment, and peace.

Reversed: You do not have a full understanding of your emotions, and thus your voice is not ready to be made manifest. You hesitate to accept yourself and how you feel. Why is this so?

II of Voice

II OF VOICE

Upright: You have gained a companion for your journey, whether that be a friend, mentor, or romantic interest. This comrade will help balance out your party, allowing you to take on greater quests.

Reversed: A grave misunderstanding has left you feeling confused about your relationship with another. Do not be afraid to voice your concerns with them and reunite.

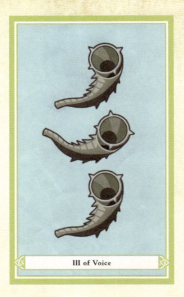

III of Voice

III OF VOICE

Upright: Your adventure will succeed; your rewards shall be abundant. Luck, fortune, victory, and more will lead to great pleasure and happiness.

Reversed: Your pleasures will turn to overindulgence, leading to strife. Know that all things must be taken in moderation. The way of the Thu'um requires balance in all things.

IV of Voice

IV OF VOICE

Upright: You grow weary of the material rewards of your adventure and now seek a greater understanding of the spiritual. Take this time to reflect. The Way of the Voice is not mastered in a day.

Reversed: You have awakened to new understanding about yourself. Now is the time to begin a new journey, start a new quest. You may even form a new relationship.

V of Voice

V OF VOICE

Upright: An unexpected loss has led to anguish, leaving you disillusioned and disappointed. Still, something remains from the ashes of your sorrow, whether it be lessons learned or greater understanding gained.

Reversed: Your joy has been replenished when it is most needed. A companion has returned to your party, or perhaps a new alliance has been formed. Your hopes will be answered in kind.

VI of Voice

VI OF VOICE

Upright: From the past may come new possibilities. A new opportunity, perhaps a new relationship, lies before you. Look toward your past acquaintances for aid or insight.

Reversed: You cling too much to your memories and worthless acquaintances. Know that the time has come to look toward future quests, not past adventures.

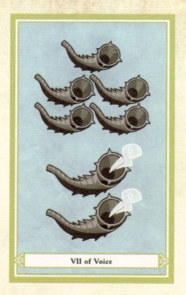

VII of Voice

VII OF VOICE

Upright: Your attention has been too scattered, and now your quest log is filled to the brim with incomplete adventures. Do not allow this illusion of success to hinder you in achieving what must be done.

Reversed: You have the will to concentrate on what is most important. Do not allow your determination to falter. Your current successes will lead to greater rewards if you keep on the path.

VIII of Voice

VIII OF VOICE

Upright: You grow weary of your quests and seek solitude. You are disappointed by your current material gains and long for a higher purpose. Take this time to reflect on what you truly want from your adventure.

Reversed: You are ready for new quests and high-tier rewards. You have abandoned the need for the spiritual and instead seek joy in the material.

IX of Voice

IX OF VOICE

Upright: Your wishes shall be granted, and rewards shall be plentiful. Whether you seek a Daedric Artifact or a work promotion, your greatest desires will become yours.

Reversed: Your wishes will not be fulfilled, and rewards will be lacking. Beware overindulgence in pleasures and misplaced trust. Your current contentment masks what you lack.

X of Voice

X OF VOICE

Upright: You have mastered the Way of the Voice, and great happiness will surely follow. Long-lasting joy, relationships, and peace are yours.

Reversed: You are at risk of losing something important, whether through your own selfishness or the betrayal of another. Be wary of those who wish you harm.

TAROT READINGS

When you enter the lands of Skyrim, you encounter so many opportunities. Will you defeat Dragons? Craft weapons? Marry, adopt, build a house? Just as the possibilities of Skyrim are infinite, so, too, are your options in how to use the tarot. You may see tarot as a ritual or simply a hobby. You may read every day or once a year. Whatever you choose, know that this deck is yours to make your own.

CARING FOR YOUR DECK

There are several ways to connect with your deck. You may do daily readings to get a feel for its energy or place it under your pillow at night. You can choose a sentimental scarf or other fabric to wrap around your deck, infusing it with your energy.

Some cleanse their decks periodically in order to purify the energy of previous readings. You may do this by passing your deck through herbal smoke, by allowing it to soak in moonlight, or through the use of crystals. Let these cleansing techniques be personal to you. When do you feel the most connected to the moon? Which herbs and crystals help you cleanse your energies? The tarot deck is an extension of you. Treat it as you would treat yourself.

PREPARING TO READ TAROT

Every tarot reading begins with a question. You may need advice on a relationship, career choice, or creative endeavor. Perhaps you simply wish to see what the next year will bring. Or perhaps you're about to fight Alduin, World-Eater and bane of kings, and want to know how best to go about it.

First, clear your mind of everything but your question. You may do so by meditating or simply closing your eyes and taking a few deep breaths. Allow the question to fill your mind, becoming your only thought. When you are fully prepared, shuffle the deck in the manner that feels most natural to you. Some choose an overhand shuffle to keep their cards from bending, while others forgo shuffling entirely and spread the cards over a large surface before selecting randomly from the pile. Do whatever feels comfortable for you.

When you feel that the time is right, draw cards and place them in a spread. A spread is a specific way of orienting your cards in order to read them. Below are a few simple spreads to get you started.

IV

The Emperor

VIII of Lockpicks

THE SPREADS

STENDARR'S INSIGHT

Stendarr, god of compassion, justice, and luck, will guide you through your simplest questions: Should I apply for this job? Will my friend forgive me? Generally, two cards upright indicate a favorable outcome, while two cards reversed signal an unfavorable outcome. As always, keep in mind your specific situation. The cards merely offer their advice. You can always change fate, should you have the resolve to do so.

1. Your first card shows your current feelings and thoughts on the situation. Use it to assess your state of being. How do you truly feel?

2. This card shows an important, but ultimately hidden, aspect of the situation. What have you not considered?

3. The last card gives you advice on how to handle the situation. Consider this card most carefully of all, for it will help guide you toward your answer.

1   2   3

ARKAY'S WILL

Who better than Arkay, god of the cycle of life and death, to show you when it is time to move on? His wisdom will allow you to divine when the time has come to let go, when to hold on, and what to look forward to in the future. Sometimes, death is only the beginning.

1. Your first card reveals what you need to end, move on from, or leave behind. This may be a person, place, or position.
2. The second card shows the reason for this ending and why a new start is needed. Reflect on this and how it coincides with your first card.
3. This card shows what you gain from letting go. Remember, leaving behind something makes room for something else. Something better.
4. Your fourth card shows you what wisdom has been gained from this experience.
5. The last card reveals what is waiting for you after this transition. Look toward what is to come, not what has been left behind. A new adventure awaits.

AKATOSH'S WISDOM

Sometimes we simply wish to remember what has been, reflect on what is, and look toward what is to come. Akatosh, the Dragon god of time, will guide your way. This spread is an excellent choice when you have no specific question in mind, but rather wish for the cards to guide you toward a better understanding of your current situation.

1 & 2. These two cards show past events that have led to your current situation, and are meant to be read as a set. Their meaning may not become clear until you finish the reading.

3. This card shows a recent event that has triggered a change.

4. This card represents your current state of being. Reflect on this card deeply, for it resides at the heart of the entire reading.

5. This card represents what direction your present course is taking. Have you chosen this direction, or are other forces at play?

6 & 7. These last two cards show your future and are meant to be read as a set. Do they signify an outcome you desire? Or do you wish to change your fate?

ABOUT THE AUTHOR

Tori Shafer is a writer and narrative designer for video games and has worked on titles such as *Elder Scrolls Online* and *Spellbreak*. Her love of games is matched only by her love of tarot, which she has been practicing since she was a child. When she's not playing games or reading tarot, she's spending time with her husband and beloved, bratty cat in their city apartment.

ABOUT THE ILLUSTRATOR

Erika Hollice is a Chicago-based illustrator who loves incorporating a touch of fantasy in her art. Her tarot card work draws influence from contemporary and classical artists alike, and is heavily influenced by her background in game art.

TITAN
BOOKS

144 Southwark Street
London SE1 0UP
www.titanbooks.com

Find us on Facebook: www.facebook.com/TitanBooks
Follow us on Twitter: @titanbooks

Published by Titan Books, London, in 2022.

Published by arrangement with Insight Editions, PO Box 3088, San Rafael,
CA 94912, USA. www.insighteditions.com

A CIP catalogue record for this title is available from the British Library.

ISBN: 9781803360645

Publisher: Raoul Goff
VP of Licensing and Partnerships: Vanessa Lopez
VP of Creative: Chrissy Kwasnik
VP of Manufacturing: Alix Nicholaeff
Editorial Director: Vicki Jaeger
Designer: Monique Narboneta Zosa
Senior Editor: Jennifer Sims
Associate Editor: Maya Alpert
Senior Production Editors: Jennifer Bentham and Jan Neal
Senior Production Manager: Greg Steffen
Senior Production Manager, Subsidiary Rights: Lina s Palma

Insight Editions, in association with Roots of Peace, will plant two trees
for each tree used in the manufacturing of this book. Roots of Peace
is an internationally renowned humanitarian organization dedicated to
eradicating land mines worldwide and converting war-torn lands into
productive farms and wildlife habitats. Roots of Peace will plant two
million fruit and nut trees in Afghanistan and provide farmers there with
the skills and support necessary for sustainable land use.

Manufactured in China by Insight Editions

10 9 8 7 6 5 4 3 2 1